J
B
ONEAL   Tallman, Edward

        Shaquille O'Neal

DUE DATE

3/96

Shaquille O'Neal

Shaquille O'Neal

By
Edward Tallman

Taking part BOOKS

DILLON PRESS
New York

Photo Credits

Front and back cover photos courtesy of AP—Wide World Photos

AP—Wide World Photos: 2, 6, 10, 21, 27, 30, 34, 38, 40, 44, 47, 48, 50, 52, 56, 61, 64

Retna Ltd.: (Moliere) 5, 17, 24, 69; (Steve Granitz) 12, 58, 66

Book design by Carol Matsuyama

Library of Congress Cataloging-in-Publication Data

Tallman, Edward.
    Shaquille O'Neal / by Edward Tallman.
       p. cm. — (Taking part)
    Includes index.
    ISBN 0-87518-637-8   0-382-24727-2 (pbk.)
    1. O'Neal, Shaquille—Juvenile literature. 2. Basketball players—United States—Biography—Juvenile literature. 3. Orlando Magic (Basketball team)—Juvenile literature. 4. Rap musicians—United States—Biography—Juvenile literature. [1. O'Neal, Shaquille. 2. Basketball players. 3. Afro-Americans—Biography.] I. Title.
    GV884.O54T35   1994
    796.323'092—dc20
    [B]   94-18182

A biography of Shaquille O'Neal, the star of the Orlando Magic basketball team and a successful rap music artist and actor.

Dillon Press
Macmillan Publishing Company
866 Third Avenue
New York, NY 10022

Maxwell Macmillan Canada, Inc.
1200 Eglinton Avenue East
Suite 200
Don Mills, Ontario M3C 3N1

Macmillan Publishing Company is part of the Maxwell Communications Group of Companies.

First Edition

Printed in the United States of America

10 9 8 7 6 5 4 3 2

Contents

Introduction

There was tension in the air as the men in somber business suits trudged into the room filled with television cameras and reporters. They were general managers, captains of the fate of the National Basketball Association (NBA) franchises they served. But their teams were the NBA's worst, having failed to make the play-offs. The managers had assembled for the lottery that would determine the order of selection for the 1992 college draft, in which promising basketball players are chosen to play for professional teams.

The NBA has come a long way since the early 1950s, when a team like the Fort Wayne Pistons traveled by bus to play the Minneapolis Lakers in a frigid little roadside auditorium. Today, clubs travel in the sleek comfort of chartered jetliners and play in splendid suburban palaces, athletic-arena theme parks with blinding light shows and piped-in

Shaq was the center of attention on the day of the NBA draft as everyone waited to see who would land the hot young talent.

rock and roll. The team left standing after the play-offs that follow a grinding 82-game regular season is coronated with the same fanfare as the Super Bowl champion or the World Series winner. More than world-class athletes, NBA players are millionaires, minicorporations in $2,500 suits attended by a retinue of agents, lawyers, accountants, and body-guards. The game's popularity soared in the 1980s largely because of the emergence of three larger-than-life stars—Magic Johnson, Larry Bird, and Michael Jordan—among the best players in American team sports.

Jordan, Johnson, and Bird were folk heroes. But by 1992 they were retiring, one by one. And so an era was end-ing as the little ball that determines the lottery rights to the draft's first selection began its trip through a maze-like chute. All drafts have prizes, players who can change a team's fortunes, but in 1992 a treasure was up for grabs—someone dazzling, someone heroic. The ball dropped out and the draft order was announced, number 10 first, then number 9, and so on. The suspense mounted until, finally, Pat Williams burst with joy like champagne when the cork is popped. A basketball savior would be joining the lowly Orlando Magic—a 7-foot 1-inch, 304-pound kid from

Louisiana State University (LSU). His name was Shaquille O'Neal. He was 20 years old.

In the time that elapsed between the lottery and the actual draft in June, Team Shaq had been thinking big. Shaq had carefully assembled a roster of star players to support him. He chose as his agent Leonard Armato, an attorney from Los Angeles, a former point guard with a short list of clients that included Kareem Abdul-Jabbar and football player Ron Lott. As his personal day-to-day assistant he picked Dennis Tracey, a former teammate at LSU and a buddy, someone he could trust. And of course Shaq had his mom and dad. They were role models and friends as well as authority figures.

As expected, Orlando's Pat Williams picked Shaq, and a contract worth $41 million over seven years was quickly negotiated and signed. Then Nike and Reebok came calling. Nike was the world's number-one athletic-shoe company, with a client roster that included Jordan, Scottie Pippen, and Charles Barkley—the NBA's biggest names. Nike wanted Shaq but seemed a little smug, treating him like a valued junior partner who would be groomed for the big corner office when Jordan and Barkley retired. Reebok, however,

Shaq proudly displays his Orlando Magic jersey.

was number two, and badly wanted Shaq: You will be the centerpiece of our entire global marketing strategy, company executives promised. It wasn't as much fun as a good rap beat, but what Shaq heard was music to his ears. Armato hammered out a contract with Reebok worth between $12 million and $20 million, depending on sales of the Shaq

Attaq line of shoes. Pepsi came knocking with $13 million in hand, and Team Shaq swung the door wide open. Huge contracts. Lucrative deals.

Shaq himself was a born showman, much like Magic Johnson. "I don't care much for players who stand out there [on the court] with stone faces, never reacting to anything," he says. And Shaq had a few surprises up his sleeve. As big as the people around him were thinking, Shaq was thinking bigger.

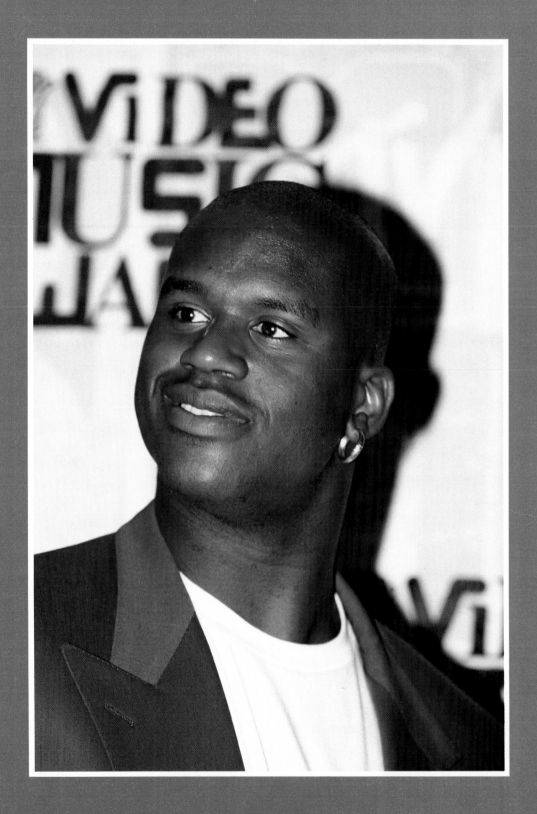

1 Little Warrior

James, Michael, Wesley, Richard—nice names for a young couple to give their first child. Solid, likable names. But too, well, *ordinary* for Lucille O'Neal and Philip Harrison, who wanted their baby boy—a 7-pound 11-ounce child, born on March 6, 1972—to have a name that stood out. A lyrical name with a percussive backbeat and music in every syllable. (Imagine Bobby Brown rapping the name: "Sha-keel!" [Bam-boom!] "O-NEAL!" [Boom-bam!]) A name that looked to the future by embracing the American present and the cultural heritage of the past. A name that declared, Behold, world: Shaquille Rashuan O'Neal.

In Arabic "Shaquille" means, ironically, "little one." "Rashuan" means "warrior." Lucille and Philip settled on O'Neal because they wanted to carry on Lucille's family name. After all, they would soon be married and might have

Shaquille's name means "little one" in Arabic, but at over 7 feet, he's anything but tiny.

more children, who could carry on the Harrison name. As it happened, they later had two girls, LaTeefah and Aesha, and a boy, Jamal, named Harrison. When Shaq was born, Lucille and Philip were living in Newark, New Jersey, a city afflicted with the social problem known as urban blight. Although Shaq's hardworking parents held city jobs, Philip with the violations bureau and Lucille in payroll, it was difficult to escape the sense of decay that was reflected in the faces of the city's poorest residents. Almost all of them were black, and they understood crime, drugs, and violence as the harsh reality of "the street"—of *their* streets. In fact, the house in which Shaq grew up on Littleton Avenue was near the desolate shells of buildings that went up in flames when blacks took to the streets after a white man assassinated Martin Luther King in the spring of 1968.

People from Shaq's neighborhood liked to say that if you breathed deeply, the smoke from the riots could still singe your lungs. Littleton Avenue wasn't the worst street in Newark, but Shaq will tell you that no episodes of TV's *Fresh Prince of Bel Air* were ever shot there, either. So, in 1974 Philip enlisted in the U.S. Army. American troops were no longer being sent to fight in Vietnam, and enlistment in the service would provide Philip's family with a semblance of financial security. More important, it gave them a way out of the 'hood.

A career in the army, though, meant that Philip Harrison would be constantly moving his family from place to place. When Shaq started elementary school, the family left Newark for Jersey City, where Shaq lived in the big, rambling house on Oak Street belonging to his doting maternal grandmother, Odessa Chamblin. Shaq's father feared that Odessa was spoiling Shaq, and he was probably relieved when the family moved to Bayonne, New Jersey, before the school year had ended. By the time Shaq was a fourth grader, he was living in Eatonton, New Jersey. Two years later, his home was in Georgia, at the Fort Stewart army base. A couple of years later, he was an army brat (the term for the children of American military-service personnel) living in Germany.

Because the family had no real hometown to serve as a fixed compass point, Shaq's life as an army brat, with its constant round of comings and goings, took its toll. Children can be cruel, especially when confronted by something that is new and different. And every time Shaq enrolled in a new school, he was taunted and jeered. Although he was extremely bright—Shaq was even able to skip first grade—kids called him dumb, thinking that because of his large size, he must have flunked a lot of grades. And his name! Just too odd, they thought, and dubbed him Sha—queer. But did Shaq hurl unkind names back at them? Or seek refuge in school authorities or solace from his parents? No. He bashed in a lot of faces.

Since he was always the biggest kid, Shaq discovered a shortcut to gaining acceptance in a new environment—just be the baddest, too. Shaq now admits he was acting like "a jerk," but at the time, being the kid who strutted around beating people up and cursing out teachers gave him an identity and made him think he was cool. And Shaq wasn't simply mischievous. He behaved like a juvenile delinquent. "People look at me now, and they think I was an angel child," Shaq says. "But I was bad. Anything before drugs and killing someone, I'd do it. I stole. I lied. I cheated. I broke into cars to steal tapes. We'd steal books out of school."

An imposing man, Sergeant Philip Harrison stood 6 feet 5 inches and weighed 250 pounds. He made a good life for

Discipline may be part of Shaq's routine now, but when he was a young man he was a real troublemaker.

his family of five, taking pride in working his way up from lowly enlisted foot soldier to drill sergeant, one of the army's most demanding jobs. Obviously, Sergeant Harrison believed in order, in a code of honor, in strict obedience to rules, and in respect for authority. He knew his son was struggling for social acceptance and that some of Shaq's unruliness stemmed from his natural exuberance. Still, his realization that his son was acting like a follower rather than a leader displeased Philip Harrison.

Shaquille's father tried to explain: Seeking acceptance and popularity, followers define themselves according to the expectations of other people. But leaders are independent and act according to what they believe to be right, following their own conscience. And until his son started acting like a leader, Philip Harrison was not going to spare the rod. Shaq recalls that he was always "too big for the strap," so his dad's "weapon of choice" was his hamlike right hand—although once Philip risked incarceration in a military jail for using a paddle.

It happened when the Harrisons were living in a housing project at the Bayonne Military Ocean Terminal in New Jersey. Shaq was instructed *never* to pull the fire alarm in the hallway unless there was a fire. One day when Shaq was hanging out with his buddies, he wondered what would happen if the alarm went off. Before long he had been carted to the station by military police. Philip burst in, brandishing a paddleball racquet. An MP reminded him that corporal punishment was against military regulations. "If you paddle that boy," he warned, "I'll have to arrest you for child abuse." Breaking a military regulation was unthinkable to Philip. Now he had to choose between the rules he was sworn to uphold and the code of conduct he had imposed on his son. He paused, and then said slowly, "You'll have to arrest me, because I'm going to beat his behind." And he did. Unwilling to arrest a fellow soldier for the offense of disciplining his son, the MP advised him, "Get out of here." Philip Harrison's philosophy of child rearing is simple. "The child does something bad on the spot, you correct him on the spot," he explains.

There were other publicly administered whippings— one in the school bathroom, after a bored Shaq had burst into a frenzy of break dancing in shop class; another for the time his father caught him strutting around showing off his jewelry and bullying a bunch of little kids. But Shaq's thuggish ways eventually gave him the scare of his life.

Shaq hated tattletales. They complicated his life, getting him into trouble with teachers—who, in turn, got him in trouble with his dad. One day in the sixth grade in Georgia, a classmate fingered Shaq as the culprit who was throwing wet toilet paper on the ceiling. After school, Shaq pounced, hitting the boy repeatedly in the stomach and face. He didn't know that his victim was epileptic. The boy fell to the ground and began to convulse. He might have died if an adult had not come along and kept him from swallowing his tongue. "This tough-guy phase is *over*," Shaq told himself. "No more fighting for me."

Shaq might have reformed then and there, but his father soon delivered the bad news. He was being transferred to Germany. Shaq's heart sank. There aren't any McDonalds on an American army base in cold, foreign, far-away Germany, he thought. Worse, there are no malls over there!

In Germany, Shaq started calling himself "J. C." (for Just Cool) and kept on acting "like a big goof," disrespecting his teachers, committing petty theft—and getting regular whippings from his exasperated father. There were drugs on the

Shaq discovered the love of his life—basketball—the first time he stepped onto a court.

base where Shaq lived, but he stayed away from users. A bright boy, Shaq feared what drugs might do to his brain. And there was the temptation of alcohol. But that, too, was a no-brainer for Shaq. One sip of beer persuaded Shaq he would just as soon drink battery acid. I can act stupid on my own if I care to, Shaq thought. I don't need help. No, Shaq did not need to be drunk or high to sustain the campaign he was waging: He thought that his out-of-control behavior would compel the army to return him to the United States. He had heard a rumor that "exile" to the States was army policy. Philip Harrison quickly disabused his son of that folly. "No way," he thundered. "I refuse to let them send you back. And as long as you act like a hooligan—I'm going to beat you every . . . single . . . day."

At the age of 13, Shaq wised up. He was tired of the beatings, and his parents promised him that rewards awaited good behavior. Moreover, Shaq can create a dramatic personality for himself. Remember, Shaq is a rapper and movie actor as well as a great athlete. He owns an explosive first step to the basket, but he can also cast himself as the hero in an imaginary world of his own making. He simply decided that being the bad guy was uncool. He was in the eighth grade now. It was time to step up and be the good guy he knew he really was. Although he made missteps once in a while, Lucille and Philip were encouraged. In learning to respect authority, Shaq was acting like a leader. And Shaq started playing basketball.

Unlike most kids who grow tall, Shaq never passed through an awkward phase. He loved music, especially rap, and he always had great dance-floor moves. In fact, he wanted to be a professional dancer like the kids on *Soul Train* or the TV series *Fame*, but his astonishing growth persuaded Shaq that his future lay elsewhere. Still, the grace he displayed in dancing gave him confidence that his innate agility could, with hard work, be transformed into superior skills in basketball.

No team sport is more fluid than hoops, or more rhythmical. The great teams of the 1980s and early 1990s can even be classified in musical terms: Larry Bird's blue-collar Boston Celtics were rock and roll; if they had a soundtrack, Bruce Springsteen should have composed it. The Los Angeles Lakers of Kareem Abdul-Jabbar and Magic Johnson were sweet soul music, a Quincy Jones production with Aretha Franklin singing and Paula Abdul (who once was a

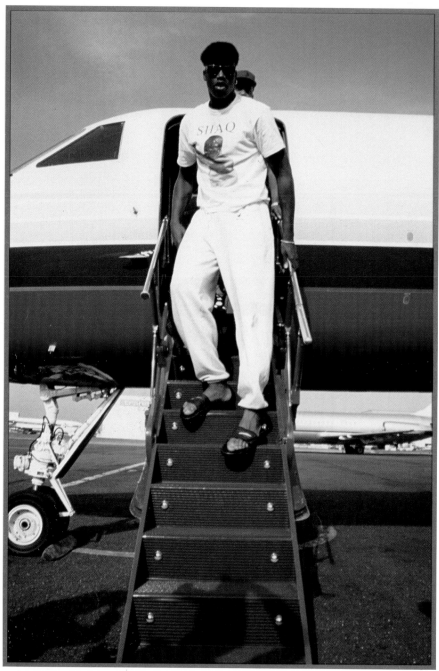

When he was a boy, Shaq traveled around the world as an army brat. Now he travels as a sports superstar.

Lakers cheerleader) creating the choreography. Isiah Thomas's Detroit Pistons—the NBA's Motor City bad boys—were gangsta rap, while His Airness Michael Jordan and the rest of the above-the-rim-soaring Chicago Bulls were hip-hop, Bobby Brown, and the hard, brassy sound of new jack swing.

A lot of NBA big men—most of them "'footers," which is Shaq's term for people standing at least 7 feet tall—lack physical grace. But the game's great centers—Wilt Chamberlain, Bill Russell, Kareem Abdul-Jabbar, Bill Walton, Patrick Ewing, Hakeem Olajuwon, and David Robinson—have combined power with magisterial athleticism. They could dunk, rebound, and intimidate in the paint, but running the floor, passing the ball, leaping, and—perhaps most important—moving without the ball are skills they have perfected as well. The great ones understand that height and strength are not enough. Standing near the basket and waiting for teammates to pass the ball will not make them winners. They have learned to position themselves by perfecting their footwork—like dancers. Magic Johnson, for example, was a 6-foot 9-inch point guard who could play any position on the floor, and he seemed to embody the quintessential rhythm of the sport. And Shaq knew that he, too, could play. He had rhythm. He could *dance*.

Shaq's first coach was his dad, who had played some junior-college ball, for Essex County College in Newark. Although Shaq was too young to have seen the famous clash-of-the-titans battles between Chamberlain and Russell in the 1960s, Philip Harrison admired Russell's great Celtics teams, and he instructed his son in the power game of the big men who had ruled in the NBA in the 1960s and 1970s—Chamberlain and Russell, of course, but also Willis Reed of the New York Knicks, Wes Unseld of the Baltimore (later Washington) Bullets, and Bob Lanier of the Pistons.

Shaq, however, was a child of the 1980s, when the NBA was dominated by perimeter players—guards like Magic Johnson, Isiah Thomas, and Michael Jordan or multitalented forwards like Larry Bird, Julius Erving, and James Worthy, who could knock down 20-foot jumpers and throw thread-the-needle passes better than most point guards. Also, Shaq was embarrassed by the way he towered over other kids his age. He tended to slouch and even tried to shrink himself on the basketball court, where he adopted a style of play better suited to a small forward than an indomitable

Shaq tries some of his smooth moves on New York Knicks center Patrick Ewing.

center. For example, his first sports idol was not the 7-foot 2-inch Abdul-Jabbar but the acrobatic Dr. J—Julius Erving of the Philadelphia 76ers—who swooped and glided and slam-dunked his way into the Hall of Fame in Springfield, Massachusetts.

Shaq also suffered from Osgood-Schlatter's disease, causing a pain in his knees that was aggravated by his rapid growth. He took calcium pills and consumed lots of milk and bananas to fight the pain, which persisted until he was in high school. Discouraged because he couldn't dunk even after attaining the height of 6 feet 8 inches—at the age of 14!—Shaq almost gave up on basketball. However, he loved the game and he had another motivation: wealth. Shaq saw how the children of army officers always had new clothes and bicycles, and he told himself: I'm gonna be richer than all these other kids. When his father saw Shaq getting lazy, he would say, "If you're gonna make it as a basketball player, you've got to eat with that basketball, you've got to sleep with that basketball." That basketball will put food on your table someday, he reminded Shaq.

In April 1987, when Shaq was finishing his sophomore year of high school, his father was transferred to the Fort

Sam Houston army base in San Antonio, Texas. The whole time he had been in Germany, Shaq had struggled "to get my skills on a par with my body," as he says in his autobiography *Shaq Attaq!* (1993). But as the pain in his knees subsided, Shaq was ready to make his presence felt in basketball, and not just in the sprawling city of San Antonio.

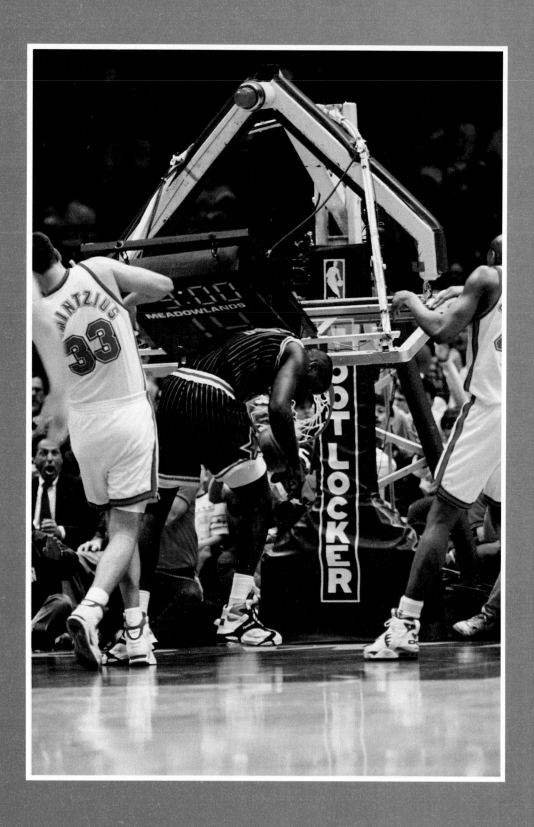

2 Back in the U.S.A.

Shaq wondered, "Should I really attend a small school—an army-base school? A 2-A [small] institution in a state where football is king and the best and biggest high schools are classified as 5-A [large]?" But his father had decided that little Robert C. Cole Junior and Senior High School was good enough. "If you're good," he told Shaq, "they'll find you." Besides, Dale Brown had already discovered Shaquille O'Neal.

A couple of years before, on the base at Wildflicken, Germany, Shaq had attended a basketball seminar given by Dale Brown, the head coach of Louisiana State University, an engaging man who always fielded competitive teams in the Southeastern Conference. After Brown's talk, Shaq asked him for a workout program that would strengthen his legs and improve his vertical leap.

"I'm 6 feet 6 inches or 6 feet 7 inches," Shaq com-

Shaq topples a backboard with a powerful dunk.

plained, "and I can't even dunk."

"How long have you been in the service, soldier?" Brown inquired.

"I'm 13; I'm not even in high school yet," Shaq explained.

"Uh—where's your dad, son?" asked Brown.

Brown stayed in touch with the Harrisons, but for the time being, Shaq reveled in being a high-school teenager in the United States. He made good grades, almost all A's and B's, with just a smattering of C's. Even though he probably broke football coach Joel Smith's heart when he decided his future on the hardwood was too important to put his knees at risk on the gridiron, Shaq served as the football team's statistician. He liked to joke with Smith that his presence on the sidelines with a clipboard gave Cole High a psychological advantage: If the statistician is 7 feet tall and weighs about 300 pounds, opponents wondered, how big are the ballplayers?

The "old" Shaq made life miserable for his teachers, but the Cole High Shaq was a teacher's pet. Mr. Jordan, his history teacher, volunteered to be the big guy's agent when he went to the NBA, and Shaq liked to play harmless pranks on

Mr. Jordan and Mr. Compton, the principal. Coach Smith became one of his pals, and he respected his basketball coach, Dave Madura. Shaq's only fight was the time he "disciplined" another student—for talking back to a teacher! The students, too, liked the happy-go-lucky big guy with the million-dollar smile and sunny personality. Of course, his popularity didn't suffer, either, when Cole High became the most feared basketball team in the entire state of Texas.

As a junior, Shaq led his team to an undefeated regular season. A Goliath among boys, he was quick and agile and had a respectable vertical leap of 28 inches. Would-be defenders desperately flailed away at this colossus who, outweighing even the largest players by almost 100 pounds, committed fouls that referees tended not to call. Pushed, shoved, crowded, and hacked at mercilessly, Shaq missed some easy shots, so he retaliated by taking the ball to the hole, slam-dunking on the heads of opponents every time Cole High needed a basket.

Years later, an NBA coach would observe that Shaq has "Larry Bird eyes," a take-no-quarter-give-no-quarter look indicating that Shaq plays to win every time he steps on the court. But as a high-school junior, he had yet to

Shaq's "killer instinct" helps him slip past opponents on the court.

develop the "killer instinct" that he now says is the true source of his greatness. He tried to emulate the playing style of Dominique Wilkins, the so-called human highlight film for the NBA's Atlanta Hawks. That was a mistake. Wilkins was an artist using the hardwood as his canvas. "Son, just take the ball to the hole and tear the basket down," advised Philip Harrison.

Having become comfortable with the physical authority he exerted on the court, Shaq at last began to understand the mental aspect of basketball. In a pickup game on the playground one day, the guy guarding Shaq unloosed a torrent of trash talk—trying to rattle Shaq, trying to trick him into mental errors. The guard, of course, wanted to compensate for physical shortcomings by gaining the psychological advantage. Although enraged, Shaq realized, "That's the book on me: Shaq's mentally 'soft'; talk to him and you can beat him." Taking a large step toward athletic maturity, he resolved to transform his anger into the physical domination of every basketball game he played.

The need for mental discipline was reinforced when Cole High was upset in the regional finals of the 1988 state basketball tournament. Shaq had stayed out late the night before and lacked concentration. He quickly got into foul trouble and missed some free throws when the game was on the line in the fourth quarter. After winning 32 consecutive games, Cole High lost to an inferior team. The season was over. Never again, Shaq thought. I'll always be a good guy off the court, but when the opening tip goes up, I shall become a warrior, a basketball ninja—the assassin of my opponent's hopes.

In the summer before his senior year, Shaq played in a couple of tournaments for emerging high-school-age stars on the basketball horizon. At the Basketball Congress Invitational in Houston, Shaq dominated a 7-footer who weighed even more than he did! And at an all-star congregation in Arizona, Shaq outplayed the guy college scouts were calling the nation's best young big man, the then-7-foot 4-inch Shawn Bradley (who later became a 7-foot 6-inch center for the 76ers). Back in San Antonio, Shaq's family mailbox was stuffed with college brochures. The leading college coaches were willing to stand in line to talk to Shaq, who was enjoying high school too much to have his senior year disrupted by an endlessly ringing telephone. He narrowed his list of prospective colleges to five schools: North

Carolina, Arizona, Illinois, North Carolina State (NC State), and LSU.

The day Dean Smith showed up smoking a cigarette in their athletic offices, Joel Smith and Dave Madura knew that Cole High was on the nation's basketball map. Dean Smith was the head coach at . . . North Carolina. Dean Smith had won a national championship, and his smooth, classy teams never cheated, never broke the rules. He was one of the sport's acknowledged spokesmen. He had discovered and coached Michael Jordan! Oh, and that rumpled fellow who slept on the couch in Joel Smith's office? That was Greg Carse, one of Dale Brown's assistants at LSU. And Jim Valvano, the colorful raconteur who had put a national championship trophy in the showcase at North Carolina State—he got so excited talking to Shaq that he spilled coffee all over Lucille O'Neal's carpet!

Philip Harrison wanted his son to go to North Carolina. The Tar Heels were always great, and Carolina was among the most prestigious universities in the South. But Harrison kept his silence. This was one of the most important decisions his son would ever make, and Shaq alone must make it. Shaquille narrowed the field to North Carolina and LSU.

Shaq goes up and up for a basket.

Carolina played in the Atlantic Coast Conference (ACC), which was probably the best conference in the country. Schools like Duke, Carolina, NC State, Maryland, and Virginia had great basketball traditions and lots of alumni in the NBA. Most of the ACC universities could boast of their reputation for academic excellence, and every year, it seemed, an ACC school was winning the national championship or playing for it in the NCAA tournament's Final Four. LSU, on the other hand, was in the Southeastern Conference (SEC), a good conference, but more likely to yield football dynasties than immortal basketball teams. Although Dale Brown had turned the LSU Tigers into a national hoops power, only Kentucky in the SEC had a basketball tradition akin to that of Duke or North Carolina.

The choice was obvious—North Carolina!—right? Wrong. Image may not be everything, but in the Shaquille order of life's highest values, it ranks up there with power slams and rap. The ACC posed an image problem for Shaq— it was a *preppie* conference. But the SEC was a place for rough-and-tumble country boys. That was a better fit for Shaq. So in November 1988 he called Coach Brown: "I'm coming to Baton Rouge." First things first, however—Shaq wanted to atone for that upset in the class 2-A regional finals the previous spring. He took his newfound killer instinct into every game and pounded the opposition. Cole High went 36-0, winning the 2-A championship in the 1989 state tournament. But even 5-A schools did not want to face Cole High School when Shaq was a senior. Over a two-year period, his teams had posted a record of 68 wins and 1 loss.

3 So Young, and So Untender

"**H**e's awesome ba-bee!" shrieked the bald man whose merry eyes and ear-to-ear smile combine improbably to make him look like a large, jovial chipmunk. "I've only got one eye, and I can see it. Shaquille O'Neal—he's the . . . real . . . DEAL BA-BEE!!"

It was December 1990, a nationally televised game between LSU and the University of Arizona, and the announcer with the annoying yet infectious patter was Dick Vitale, college basketball's self-appointed master of ceremonies, a courtside hypemeister whom fans have come to love. He inspires ambivalence in fans, while journalists look askance at him, but Vitale is a constant in the ever-changing scenery of college basketball. And the man has an eye for talent. Anyone can watch Michael Jordan and see that he is gifted, but Vitale can spot a diamond in the rough, and he knew he had seen basketball's future when he first laid

In college, Shaq picks up an award for his awesome playing. **41**

Shaquille O'Neal

eyes on the teenage Shaquille O'Neal. College basketball players are fond of Vitale, so Shaq paid attention when Vitale sauntered into the LSU dressing room and asked the big guy to make it an entertaining game. "Your team doesn't have much chance of winning today," Vitale somberly declared.

Arizona had the best front line in the country in Sean Rooks, a 6-foot 11-inch forward; Brian Williams, a 6-foot 11-inch center-forward; and silky smooth 6-foot 8-inch forward Chris Mills. "Everybody thinks we're gonna lose," Shaq told his teammates before the game. "Let's go out and play hard and show them different." Shaq got into early foul trouble and had to ride the bench for long stretches. Late in the game, he scanned the bleachers, catching his mother's eye. "Take over," she mouthed. In the last few minutes of the game, Shaq swatted three shots by Rooks and seemed to persuade Williams that it was illegal in Louisiana to play in the paint against the Shaq, who quickly scored 16 of his game-high 29 points, snared 10 of his 14 rebounds, and broke open a close game that—surprise, Mr. Vitale—LSU won 92-82. "The tapes don't do Shaq justice," Chris Mills said. "It's kind of amazing to see him in person."

So Young, and So Untender

Shaq had arrived in Baton Rouge in the fall of 1989 fully grown to his adult height of 7 feet 1 inch. He tipped the scales at 295 pounds, and notwithstanding his almost nutrient-free diet of pizza and fast-food burgers, Shaq's body fat count was low. Consider that the original 'footer, Wilt Chamberlain, the most powerful force in NBA history, had entered the professional ranks in 1959 at a weight of 265, and you begin to understand why Shaq says that no single individual can stop him one-on-one.

As a freshman, Shaq had maintained a 2.9 grade point average, the best on the team, but he did not step forward as the LSU leader on the court, largely because of the presence of two veteran players, guard Chris Jackson and 7-foot forward Stanley Roberts. Jackson was a guard who preferred shooting to passing. He wasn't eager to create opportunities for his teammates to score, and Roberts had never seen a shot he didn't like. Although playing in an every-man-for-himself offense hampered his development, Shaq played the role of rebounder and shot blocker, and LSU posted a regular season record of 23-7. However, Coach Brown's heavily favored Tigers lost to Auburn in the first round of the SEC tournament and were eliminated

Playing for Arizona, Shaq gets into a rumble with an opponent.

from postseason play by Georgia Tech in the second round of the NCAA tournament.

Minus Chris Jackson and Stanley Roberts, LSU won 20 of 30 games in 1990-1991 and finished the regular season with a share of the SEC championship. Although a hairline fracture of his left leg hurt LSU's chances in tournament play and caused him to miss 2 games, Shaq blossomed in his sophomore season. He was the nation's leading rebounder (14.7 a game) and seventh-best scorer (27.6 per game), had a field-goal percentage of 62.8, and was third in the country in blocked shots. He made every all-America team that mattered, and the Associated Press named him Player of the Year. (Shaq was only the fifth sophomore to capture that honor; the others were Kareem Abdul-Jabbar [then Lew Alcindor], Bill Walton, Ralph Sampson, and Mark Aguirre.) LSU fans chanted, "Two more years, two more years," but passing on the NBA meant another year of dormitory food and saying no to millions of dollars. Still, Shaq's parents wanted him to grow emotionally before turning professional, and Shaquille agreed. Another year at LSU can't hurt me, he reasoned; and declaring for the NBA only for the money wouldn't be a wise decision.

Shaquille O'Neal

Shaq was again unanimously named to the all-American teams, but his junior year "just wasn't fun," he says. The team was split by dissension and jealousy; some younger players resented Shaq's celebrity and the fact that he was LSU's main man. Moreover, Shaq was tired of being double- and triple-covered in every game, and the referees were letting defenders mug him on the court. He held his temper in check until the Tennessee game in the second round of the SEC tournament. LSU was coasting to victory when a Volunteer player almost tackled Shaq, attempting to prevent an easy lay-in. Because the tactic could have injured him, Shaq threw a vicious elbow that grazed the guy's face. Pandemonium erupted. Both benches emptied, fights broke out all over the court, and even Dale Brown jumped into the fray.

"When Coach Brown got out there, it got really crazy," Shaq recalls. The officials ejected Shaq, and he was suspended for the tournament championship game between Kentucky and LSU. Without Shaq, LSU lost but still made the 64-team NCAA tournament field. The Tigers beat Brigham Young before being eliminated by Indiana in the second round, despite 36 points, 12 rebounds, and 5

Shaq slams one home during an all-American team game.

In 1991 Shaq received the Associated Press Player of the Year award.

blocked shots by Shaq. In three years Shaq had helped his team win two regular-season SEC championships, but he had not come close to making the Final Four, which had been his dream. Even Dale Brown thought that turning pro might be best for Shaq. In the NBA, zone defenses are illegal; three and four defenders wouldn't be draped over him like an ill-fitting suit every time he touched the ball.

When Shaq encounters stress, he jumps in his Jeep, pumps up the volume on the stereo to a windshield-shattering decibel level, and just drives and chills, letting rap beats free his body and ease his state of mind. A couple of days after the Indiana loss, Shaq set off at midnight, driving straight through from Baton Rouge to San Antonio, to talk to his parents. He liked Dale Brown, but the coaching at LSU was not helping him improve on all phases of his game. He was tired of selfish, backbiting teammates and fed up with opposing players trying to hurt him because they could not stop him. He was ready for the NBA. However, Lucy O'Neal, whom Dale Brown calls an "absolute saint," wanted her son to have a diploma first and a fat bank account second. "When I got out of high school," she explains, "I told myself I would go to college, but I got mar-

Shaq shakes hands with an admiring fan—former president George Bush.

ried young and I chose to stay home with the children. I enjoyed that, but I've always regretted not getting that college degree. I know there's all that money out there, but I want him to have that diploma so he'll have something real to depend on."

At the tender age of 20, Shaq would enter the NBA as the most ballyhooed rookie since the arrival of Larry Bird and Magic Johnson in 1979, and his untender power would make him basketball's greatest physical force since Wilt Chamberlain. And Lucy O'Neal had no need to worry. Her son had something besides athletic ability to depend on: charisma—the kind of movie- and rock-star charisma— that gives Shaq youth-culture credibility beyond the reach even of Michael Jordan and Charles Barkley.

4 Don't Fake the Funk

February 3, 1993. The fans' ballots for the upcoming NBA All-Star game had been tabulated, and Pat Riley was seething. Dapper Pat Riley, the master motivator with the film-star looks and fashion-plate wardrobe, who had coached the Los Angeles Lakers to four world titles in the 1980s and now had his New York Knicks in the hunt for the NBA championship. But Riley was complaining bitterly to the media about what he considered a travesty: Patrick Ewing, the perennial All-Pro center for the Knicks, an eight-year veteran who had played on the Dream Team at the 1992 Olympic Games and who had the best outside jump shot of any center ever, Patrick Ewing— Riley's go-to guy, for goodness' sake—would be riding the bench at the All-Star game behind a rookie. Behind Shaquille O'Neal! Even if the power to compel a new vote had been Riley's to wield, it would have been pointless.

As he prepares to sink a perfect dunk, Shaq seems to hang in the air. **53**

Shaquille O'Neal

Shaq had been named on 826,767 ballots, receiving almost 300,000 votes more than Ewing. Only Michael Jordan, Charles Barkley, and Scottie Pippen—all of them established Dream Team superstars—had outpolled the Orlando Magic's rookie phenomenon. The fans had spoken: Patrick was great, but it was Shaquille they really wanted to see.

When the NBA season had started in the fall of 1992, fans and journalists alike were asking: Could the league sustain the popularity it had enjoyed in the 1980s now that both Larry Bird and Magic Johnson had retired? Could Michael Jordan lead his Chicago Bulls to a third consecutive league title? Could Shaquille O'Neal possibly live up to his advance billing? And if so, could he fill some of the void left by the absence of Bird and Johnson? By season's end, each of those questions was answered with an emphatic *yes*!

How best to measure Shaq's rookie year? Victories. When Kareem Abdul-Jabbar was picked first in the 1969 draft, he turned his team around. The Milwaukee Bucks went from 27 wins in 1968-1969 to 56 victories with Abdul-Jabbar in 1970. In 1978 the Lakers won 47 games; a year later, with Magic Johnson in the lineup, Los Angeles won 60 contests and an NBA title. San Antonio had lost 61 games the year before David Robinson joined the team, but with "the Admiral" in the lineup in 1989-1990, the Spurs won 56. And how did the Orlando Magic fare? The team had the league's second-worst record in the Shaq-less 1991-1992 season, losing 61 of 82 games. O'Neal carried Orlando to a .500 season—41 wins, 41 losses—and the team came within an eyelash of making the play-offs. Moreover, Shaq was among the league's leaders in scoring (24 points a game), rebounding (14 a game), and blocked shots (almost 4 per outing). He recorded the league's fourth-best field-goal percentage, and his 322 dunks stand as an unofficial NBA record.

A better measure of Shaq's contribution may be that the once-lowly Orlando Magic, an expansion team that did not exist before 1989, was the league's second-leading road draw behind the world-champion Chicago Bulls. Shaq has been worth every penny of his $41 million contract. He and Michael Jordan led the league in putting fans in the stands. Like Jordan, Magic, and Bird, Shaq is a franchise player, someone who revolutionizes the game and astonishes even jaded observers, who gives his all and then, improbably, finds hidden reserves that inspire his team and deflate

Shaq fools around with Patrick Ewing as they warm up for the 1993 NBA All-Star game.

opponents' hopes. A franchise NBA player makes people say on a bitter winter evening, "Bundle up—we're going to the game!"

Professional basketball has enjoyed two golden eras—the 1960s, when Bill Russell's Boston Celtics ruled the league; and the 1980s, when Larry Bird's Celtics and Magic Johnson's Lakers fought for supremacy, and Michael Jordan was becoming the greatest player in the history of American team sports. But in the 1960s and 1970s, superstars like Jerry West, Oscar Robertson, and Elgin Baylor were measured simply by their quality of play. They emboldened teammates, played hard defense, scored almost at will, and, most important, demanded the ball at crunch time, when the game was on the line. They made the Hall of Fame and cast long shadows over the game of basketball. The familiar player on the NBA logo is a silhouette of Jerry West.

In the 1990s, however, airtime means a music video/shoe commercial in regular rotation on the tube, not a gravity-defying leap by Michael Jordan. Players align themselves with sneaker and soft-drink companies the way satellite nations in the cold war sided with the Soviet Union or the United States. (Jordan and Barkley are Nike; Shaq is

Because of Shaq's status as a role model and sports hero, he's in big demand as a spokesperson for a variety of products, from soft drinks to sneakers.

Reebok. The U.S. men's Olympic basketball team is Coca-Cola, but Shaq is Pepsi; thus, Shaq was not a member of Olympic Dream Team II until organizers were forced to recognize his skill and popularity and finally named him to the team in March 1994.) Obscurity is the fate of players without clout in the marketplace, and NBA All-Stars are media celebrities beyond the realm of sports. "It used to be that the personality cult was reserved for movie stars and rock performers," explains a Reebok executive. "But for kids, what is cool is now being determined by athletes." Even David Stern, the commissioner who presides over the league, has compared the NBA to Walt Disney. "They have theme parks," he says. "We have theme parks. Only we call them 'arenas.' They have characters: Mickey Mouse, Goofy. Our characters are named Magic and Michael. Disney sells apparel. We sell apparel. They make home videos. We make home videos."

Shaq's media-savvy agent, Leonard Armato, explains that the NBA is a "marketing partner [of Brand Shaq] on a level with Reebok." Indeed, O'Neal is pro basketball's first multimedia celebrity. His signature power jam—the most violent in the history of the game—especially excites young fans, the ones who admired Jordan but consider Shaq the player of their generation. But Shaq's power game is augmented by showmanship and dramatic flair. For example, in a nationally televised Sunday-afternoon game on February 7, 1993, between the Orlando Magic (it was the team's first-ever appearance on network TV) and Charles Barkley's Phoenix Suns, Shaq dunked early in the first quarter, pulling the basket to the floor and toppling the huge stanchion that supports the backboard! That volcanic slam probably inspired impressionable fans to conceive of Shaq as a cartoon superhero become flesh. And Leonard Armato, who had declared Shaq a "cross between The Terminator and Bambi" when his client was drafted, said, "Shaq is an action hero who doesn't need special effects."

In December 1992, during a West Coast road swing by the Magic, Shaq made his national debut as a rapper on *The Arsenio Hall Show,* performing "Can We Rock? Yeah, What's Up Doc?" with Fu Schnickens, the Brooklyn-based group whose members are Shaq's favorite rappers. Shaq is a hard rapper, and "Can We Rock?" celebrated the way Shaq rocks on the basketball court and Fu Schnickens rocks as MCs. Late in 1993, Shaq released his first album, *Shaq Diesel,*

Shaq works the audience during a performance of his rap music.

with more raps about his hoops prowess, such as "(I Know I Got) Skillz" and lyrics like "First draft pick and now it's time for me to fulfill my dream/To be in the league and slam like Hakim." Chalk up another first for Shaq. He also leads the NBA in rap albums.

Is there a medium Shaq has yet to conquer? Film? Shaq is the only professional athlete to share star billing with Nick Nolte in a major Hollywood movie. William Friedkin, who directed *The French Connection* and *The Exorcist*, had been impressed with O'Neal's "enormous likability" when he saw the popular Reebok commercial starring Shaq and the game's legendary retired centers—Chamberlain, Russell, Abdul-Jabbar, and Walton—that aired for the first time during Super Bowl XXVII in January 1993. The spot opens with Shaq seeking admission to the Place of Basketball Immortals. He approaches the door, and Bill Russell tersely asks him for the password. "Don't fake the funk on a nasty dunk," answers Shaq.

That line has become the best-known retort in recent advertising history, and it was a Shaq original. The script called for him to say, "Speak softly and carry a big stick." "That's wack, bro'," Shaq protested. "I'd never say anything corny like that." The producers changed it to "Speak softly and carry a big game." Still wack. So Shaq improvised. The result? For Reebok, a memorable TV spot; for Shaq, a key role in a film by Friedkin, who saw that the young superstar had personality and a commanding physical presence on the screen even when he wasn't power jamming.

Shaq is effective in front of the camera because he maintains his composure. He seems loose and relaxed in his Reebok and Pepsi commercials. Also, Shaq explains, "I've got great facial expressions." In *Blue Chips* (1994)—the title refers to the term for can't-miss high-school athletic prospects—Shaq is charming and effective in the role of Deon Boudreaux, a basketball natural, a raw but unstoppable talent from Louisiana who is recruited by the coach (Nick Nolte) of the Western University Dolphins, a once-powerful program that has fallen on losing times. "He's so savvy," gushes Friedkin. "[Shaq] could have a huge career in anything he wants." With an insightful script by Ron Shelton, who wrote two other noted sports films, *Bull Durham* and *White Men Can't Jump*, *Blue Chips* was marketed as a comedy and sports-action movie. While *Chips* did feature numerous O'Neal slam dunks and feathery long-

Shaq hangs out on the set of Blue Chips.

range jumpers by Anfernee Hardaway (of the Orlando Magic), the film is really about the interior drama of the coach, an ethical man who despises himself when Western U. alumni start buying talented youngsters like gaudy tree ornaments at Christmastime.

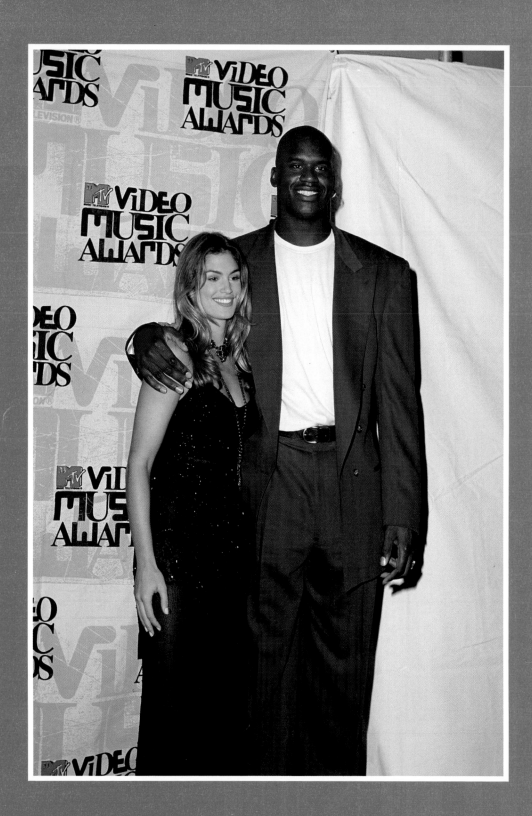

5 The Future Is Now!

When Michael Jordan retired from basketball in the fall of 1993, Charles Barkley and 21-year-old Shaquille O'Neal suddenly became the NBA's most famous and charismatic active players. Barkley, however, has a painful chronic back injury and will probably retire after the 1993-1994 season. Shaq will then become the league's unofficial international ambassador, a role Jordan never wanted but O'Neal seems to relish, as did Magic Johnson. But even more than Barkley, Jordan, and Johnson, Shaq, with his recordings and movies, is equipped to carry the NBA message to a new, global generation of fans. And whereas Charles Barkley has said, "I am *not* a role model—*parents* should be role models," Shaq feels that, like it or not, he influences people's behavior. Celebrity has made him a role model. Nevertheless, Shaq is sympathetic to Barkley's point of view. In his video *Shaq Attaq: In Your Face*

Cindy Crawford and Shaq pose at the MTV Video Music Awards.   **67**

(1993), he said, "I think the real hero in my life is my dad," and Shaq knows that when a child asks, "Why should I refuse drugs?" parents must have the answers.

In the 1993 off-season, while filming *Blue Chips,* Shaq became friends with Anfernee Hardaway, who left school early for the NBA. Pat Riley calls Hardaway, a 6-foot 7-inch guard, the "second coming of Magic Johnson," and in June the Orlando Magic staged yet another draft-day coup by landing the multitalented Hardaway. Giving the Magic team a steady perimeter game, Hardaway joined Shaq's already promising supporting cast of young players—Nick Anderson, Scott Skiles, and Dennis Scott. While the Magic didn't take the Eastern Conference's Atlantic Division title for the 1993-1994 season, Shaq led the league in scoring with a 28.7-points-per-game average, and he was connecting on more than 60 percent of his field-goal attempts. He was also among the NBA leaders in rebounds, in blocked shots, and in two important unofficial categories—intimidation in the paint and coverage in the electronic and print media.

Shaq may be the most dominant player in the league now, but he is not the NBA's most complete player. That

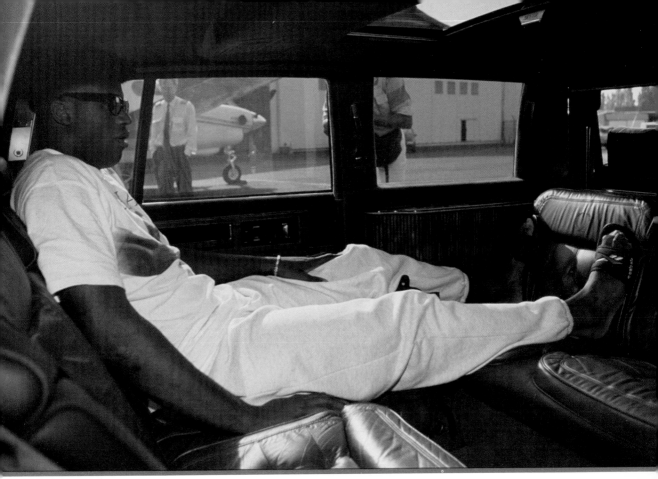

The king of the basketball court relaxes in his limo.

honor would go to Chicago's Scottie Pippen or San Antonio's David Robinson. Shaq knows he must improve his game. He commits too many turnovers—in his rookie year he traveled with the ball 74 times, the most walking violations in the league, and also led the league in offensive fouls, with 48—and must increase his assist-to-turnover ratio, although he has the tools and intelligence to become a fine passer. His most glaring weakness is free-throw shooting. Wilt Chamberlain was ridiculed for his lifetime percentage of 51 at the line, and Shaq is little better, hitting foul shots at an abysmal rate of 59 percent in his first season. He must become proficient at the charity stripe if he is to be the Magic's go-to guy in the fourth quarter of close games.

At the NBA All-Star game in Minneapolis on February 13, 1994, Shaq again started at center for the East team, ahead of Patrick Ewing. Shaq had a hit rap album in the stores, and the opening of *Blue Chips* in theaters across the nation was just five days away. A lot of NBA players resent the attention he has received so early in his career— the acclaim, the magazine covers, the commercials, the recordings, the way he has announced, "No tomorrows, bro'. I am *the man* in this league right *now*!" Shaq wanted to dominate in the All-Star contest, a game not known as a showcase for bruising defensive play, but the West big men—David Robinson, Hakeem Olajuwon, Karl Malone, and Shawn Kemp—double- and tripled-covered Shaq every time he touched the ball. He didn't score a dunk until late in the game and overall made just 2 of 12 shots from the floor. Providing color analysis of the game for NBC, Magic Johnson said, "Shaquille needs to develop a go-to shot from more than 2 feet away from the basket. [My Lakers teammate] Kareem had the skyhook. He could shoot it even with two or three men guarding him. Shaq needs to have that kind of weapon. In the play-offs, defenses will sag on him and take away his dunk."

Bill Walton agrees with Magic. "Shaq owes it to himself and to the game of basketball to expand his game," he declares. However, Shaq's detractors believe that he is spread too thin, that he pays more attention in the off-season to his burgeoning recording and film careers than to improving his game. Certainly, if he plays someday for a team that wins an NBA title, his place in basketball history will be secured. But does Shaq have the discipline and desire to leave footprints in the sand alongside those of Abdul-Jabbar, Russell, Chamberlain, and Walton? "Someday I'll be a legend, like Bird and Magic and Jordan," he says. "I'll be there one day. It takes time."

And time is on Shaq's side.

Index